2 The *Mary Celeste's* crew and their journey

The captain of the *Mary Celeste* was Benjamin Briggs, a very experienced sailor. He was sailing with his wife, Sarah, and their two-year-old daughter, Sophia.

They **set sail** with seven other **crew** members from New York City on 7 November 1872. The ship was heading for Genoa in Italy, which meant they had to cross the whole of the Atlantic Ocean.

My ship, the *Dei Gratia*, was travelling the same route, but we set off eight days after the *Mary Celeste*.

The first few weeks of our journey were hard. The weather was stormy and there were **gale-force** winds. But we were used to that in November in the Atlantic. We know that Captain Briggs and the crew of the *Mary Celeste* also had to battle through these treacherous conditions.

3 Finding the *Mary Celeste*

We first spotted the *Mary Celeste* on the afternoon of 5 December 1872.

I was puzzled because the ship looked out of control.

But there were no **distress signals** and, after watching her for a while, we decided to take a closer look.

We sailed close, around 300 metres away, and called out to the ship. We got no answer. There was nobody on **deck** and the sails were ripped and some were missing.

I sent three of my men over to the *Mary Celeste* in a small boat. Two of them went aboard.

They found no one there. The crew had disappeared!

I went to see for myself. The only sound was the wind whistling through the torn sails. It was very strange.

What we found on board the *Mary Celeste*

1. All of the **cargo** was still there – except for nine barrels that were empty. The crew's personal belongings were also still on board.

2. We checked the **ship's log** and the final entry was at 8 o'clock in the morning on 25 November 1872. That was ten days earlier!

Their position then was near the island of Santa Maria in the Azores and land was in sight. That is when the crew must have left the ship.

The *Mary Celeste* had sailed more than 700 kilometres on her own!

Did you know?

700 kilometres is even further than the distance between London in England and Edinburgh in Scotland. A long way to sail with no crew!

nautical
miles = about
1 kilometres

Date: 25 November 1872
Time: 8:00 a.m.
Position: 37° 01' N 25° 01' W
Six miles south of Santa Maria Island
Course: E by NE
Speed:
Weather:
Remarks: Saw the island distinctly

These two entries had not been filled in.

3. There was nearly a metre of sea water in the hold – that would have come up past my waist!

That is quite a lot of water for a small ship to take in, but not enough to sink it.

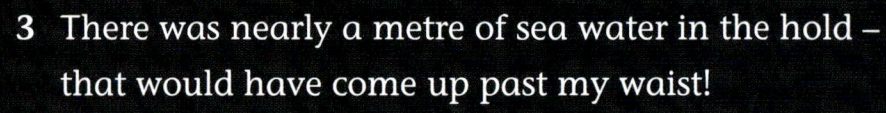

4 One of the pumps that is used to remove water was lying on the deck. It had been taken apart – perhaps because it was broken.

5 Also lying on the deck was the "sounding rod" – this is a stick you dip in a stream to see how deep the water is. On a ship, the sounding rod is used to see how much water is in the hold – the bottom of the ship.

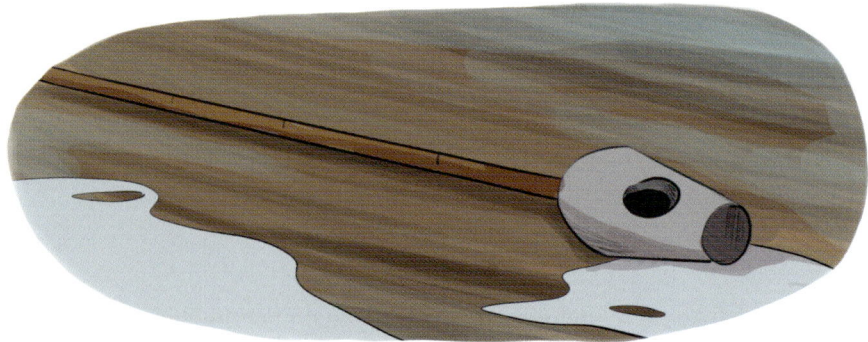

6 There were no signs of a disturbance or a fire.

7 In the **galley** everything was soaking wet from seawater. But there was enough food and drinking water to last six months.

8 Two of the ship's three hatches were open. A hatch is like a door or lid on the deck and they are kept closed to keep rain and seawater from getting in. So, because they were open, the middle decks of the *Mary Celeste* were soaking wet, including the captain's bedroom.

What was missing?

Most of the ship's papers, equipment to help the crew find their way at sea and – most importantly – the **lifeboat** were nowhere to be found. The crew must have used it to leave the ship.

What does all of this tell us?

The ship had taken in water, but one of the pumps may not have been working. That would have made it more difficult to remove that water.

The sounding rod was on the deck, instead of in a safe dry space. This shows that one of the last things the crew did was to check how much water was in the ship.

We know that land was in sight and, whatever happened, it took place in the morning. So when the crew of the Mary Celeste set off in the lifeboat, they thought they could make it to safety.

But they took only a few things with them, so they probably left in a hurry.

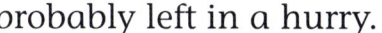

The question we need to try to solve is: why did the crew leave?

4 Idea 1: Was it a seaquake?

Seaquakes are like earthquakes, but at sea. And they can come from nowhere. One minute you're happily sailing, and the next, the whole ship starts shaking so fiercely that you fear your teeth will fall out. Your brain is screaming at you: ABANDON SHIP! Before it sinks!

If the *Mary Celeste* had run into a seaquake and taken in a lot of water, Captain Briggs would have almost certainly used the sounding rod to see how much. And if one of the pumps had broken, he might have panicked and thought the *Mary Celeste* was about to sink!

He wanted to save his family and the crew and so he might have ordered them to leave in the lifeboat *immediately*.

Maybe Captain Briggs had planned to wait nearby in the lifeboat and return to the *Mary Celeste* when he felt it was safe. But then maybe the lifeboat got separated from the ship, never to find it again.

What do you think? Was the *Mary Celeste* struck by a seaquake and the crew abandoned ship?

5 Idea 2: Was it food poisoning?

Now, I've had some bad food while at sea. Really bad!

But I've never had what they call food poisoning. That's where something has made the food so awful that, if you eat it, it will make you unwell.

It's possible the crew of the *Mary Celeste* ate something that made them sick and confused.

But what could they possibly have eaten?

There is a **mould** that can grow on flour. If it is eaten, this mould can make people see and hear things that aren't really there! Like having a bad dream, but when you're awake!

When people are confused like this, they sometimes make strange decisions. So, it's possible the crew thought they *had to* leave their big, safe ship and jump into their small lifeboat.

But …

... when we boarded the ship, all the food looked fine. There were no signs that anyone had been sick. The crew were very experienced and would probably know if food had gone bad. And if YOU felt poorly, where would you go? To bed, or into a tiny boat on the ocean?

Did you know?
Lots of sailors in the 1800s believed in mermaids. Sometimes, they mistook seals for mermaids!

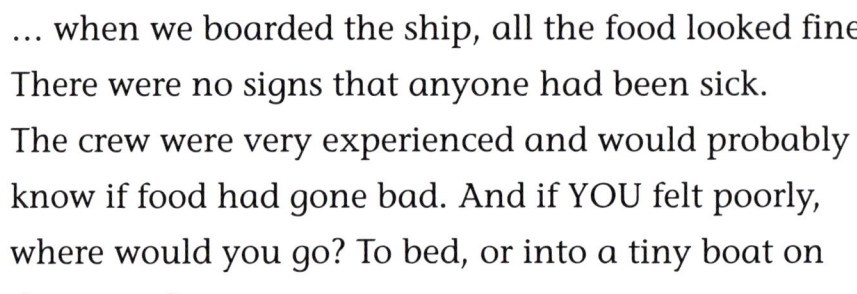

What do you think? Did the crew get food poisoning? Did they leave the ship because they were confused and thought they saw mermaids?

6 Idea 3: Was it a sea monster?

Some people believe the unfortunate crew were snatched right off the deck of the *Mary Celeste* by a giant sea monster!

I know what you're thinking. There's no such thing as sea monsters.

But there is! And I've seen one!

Did you know?
Many sailors are very superstitious. They never say "goodbye" when leaving a port. They say "fair winds" instead. And sailors don't eat bananas on board – they think this fruit brings bad luck. And they also believe in sea monsters!

In the middle of the Atlantic Ocean, I once spotted a giant squid … and I mean GIANT.

Imagine an octopus with tentacles as long as a ship's **mast** is tall. And a mouth so large it could swallow a person whole.

Those tentacles have powerful suction cups – perfect for grabbing hold of prey. Giant squid are super strong and can strike surprisingly quickly. So, it's possible!

But …

Could a sea monster *really* have seized an entire crew at once?

And remember: the lifeboat was missing, which means the crew probably left in it, rather than being grabbed by a sea creature. Unless of course, the sea monster ate that as well!

> **What do you think?** Did a sea monster attack the *Mary Celeste*?

7 Idea 4: Was it a waterspout?

Another interesting fact was how much sea water was in the middle section of the ship.

This water had got in through the open hatches above. And it almost certainly came from a storm. Possibly even a waterspout.

A waterspout is a **tornado** at sea – and, like seaquakes, they are terrifying when you are caught in the middle of one.

They are a vicious whirling column of wind and water. They vary in size from a metre to a kilometre or more in height. And the wind inside can blow at more than 160 kilometres per hour.

So, if the *Mary Celeste* was struck by a waterspout, it would have filled the middle decks with lots of water.

Again, the crew might have panicked, thinking the ship was about to sink!

They might have quickly gathered a few possessions and left the *Mary Celeste* in the lifeboat.

What do you think? Was the *Mary Celeste* struck by a waterspout?

8 Idea 5: Was it extra-terrestrial creatures?

Some people believe in life on other planets. And they say that these creatures from distant galaxies have ships that fly through space faster than a bolt of lightning. The same people might say the only explanation for the entire crew of the *Mary Celeste* going missing is KIDNAP!

But not any old kidnap, like by pirates. No, they were kidnapped by extra-terrestrials. And carried off to outer space in one of their special ships.

I must admit it all sounds unlikely to me.

And one other thing puzzles me. The space creatures would have taken the lifeboat as well as the crew. Why would they want that?

> **What do you think?** Were the crew kidnapped by creatures from another planet?

9 Idea 6: Was it an explosion?

Another idea is there was an explosion on board the *Mary Celeste*.

We know that nine of the 1701 barrels of chemicals were empty.

When the chemicals leaked out, they would have given off dangerous smells, like invisible gas. If this gas touched a flame, it would have caused a fire.

We also know that the hatches were open. Maybe they were opened by the crew to try to get rid of the dangerous smells. Or maybe the hatches were blown off in a huge explosion!

If there had been a HUGE EXPLOSION, Captain Briggs would have been worried that the ship might have caught on fire. And so he would have ordered his crew to leave in the lifeboat.

Even if there was no explosion, Captain Briggs might have been worried about the **fumes** and ordered an **evacuation**, planning to return when the smells had cleared.

Maybe he tied the lifeboat to the *Mary Celeste* but the rope snapped or came unhooked. And the ship sailed away.

But when we went aboard the *Mary Celeste*, we saw no signs of a fire or an explosion.

What do you think?
Do you think there was an explosion or that the captain thought the ship was about to blow up?

10 Idea 7: What about me?

7 November 1872
- The *Mary Celeste*, under Captain Benjamin Briggs, sets sail from New York, US, for Genoa, Italy

15 November 1872
- The *Dei Gratia*, under Captain David Morehouse, departs from New Jersey, US, for Europe

25 November 1872
- The last log entry on the *Mary Celeste*

5 December 1872
- The *Dei Gratia* spots the *Mary Celeste* about 700 kilometres west of Portugal. The ship is abandoned, with no sign of the crew or lifeboat

6 December 1872
- Sailors from the *Dei Gratia* decide to sail the *Mary Celeste* to Gibraltar

12 December 1872
- The *Dei Gratia* arrives in Gibraltar

13 December 1872
- The *Mary Celeste* arrives in Gibraltar

17 December 1872
- The Court in Gibraltar opens an investigation into the mystery of the abandoned *Mary Celeste*

Some people think I was involved in this mystery. Let me explain why …

The *Mary Celeste* and its cargo were worth a lot of money. If a ship is found abandoned, the captain who finds it gets "salvage rights" – a reward for rescuing it.

That's what happened here. Three of my crew mended the torn sails and sailed the *Mary Celeste* to Gibraltar, on the southern tip of Spain. I and three others sailed the *Dei Gratia* there. It was hard work with half a crew, but we knew the reward would be worth it.

When we arrived, there was a huge investigation to find out what had happened to the *Mary Celeste*. Nobody could work it out. But the judge said he didn't think my crew or I had done anything wrong. And we were eventually paid salvage rights.

Some people say I made a deal with Captain Briggs to share the reward money. They say I put him and the crew in a lifeboat near shore and planned to meet him later.

But that's impossible. Captain Briggs was the most honest man I've ever met. He would never abandon his ship or spend the rest of his days hiding away.

> **What do you think?**
> Do you think Captain Morehouse did it?

Did you know?
The crew of the *Mary Celeste* were never found. But the ship sailed on. It survived another 13 years, until it was run into some rocks off the coast of Haiti and was smashed to pieces by the sea. What a sad end to such a famous ship.

Glossary

cargo	goods (things to sell) that a ship carries
crew	the sailors on board a ship
deck	the floor of a ship
distress signals	ways to call for help
evacuation	quickly leaving a place to stay safe
fumes	bad or dangerous smells
gale-force	extremely strong wind
galley	the kitchen on a ship
lifeboat	a small boat carried on a bigger boat to be used in an emergency
mast	the tall pole on a ship that holds the sails up
mould	fuzzy green or black stuff that grows on stale food or any damp or humid area
nautical miles	a measure used for distances at sea. 1 nautical mile is equal to almost 2 kilometres

set sail   to begin a journey by sea

ship's log   a diary to record how far the ship has travelled and the weather conditions

tornado   spinning column of air stretching from a thundercloud down to the ground

Index

Atlantic Ocean 2, 4–6, 30

Captain Benjamin Briggs 4, 6–7, 22–23, 39, 40, 42–43

Captain David Reed Morehouse 2–3, 40–43

Dei Gratia 5, 40–41

extra-terrestrials 34–35

Genoa 5, 40

giant squid 30–31

Gibraltar 40–41

New York 5, 40

Discuss the arguments for and against each of the ideas

Ideas for reading

Written by Gill Matthews
Primary Literacy Consultant

Reading objectives:
- be introduced to non-fiction books that are structured in different ways
- discuss and clarify the meanings of words, linking new meanings to known vocabulary
- answer and ask questions

Spoken language objectives:
- participate in discussion
- speculate, hypothesise, imagine and explore ideas through talk
- ask relevant questions

Curriculum links: Geography: Geographical skills and fieldwork; History: Events beyond living memory

Word count: 2594

Interest words: narrator, abandoned, fateful, experienced, treacherous

Resources: paper, pencils and crayons, atlas

Build a context for reading

- Explore the front cover of the book with the children, discussing the image and the title.
- Discuss what they think the mystery might be.
- Read the back cover blurb. Ask how this has helped them to develop their thoughts about the book.
- Point out that this is an information book. Discuss what children know about non-fiction and what typical features they could expect to find in the book.
- Give children time to skim through the book, finding the features they have named.

Understand and apply reading strategies

- Read pp2–7 aloud.
- Ask children why certain words and phrases are in bold. Give them time to look up the words in the glossary.

1 Meet the narrator: Captain Morehouse

It was a cold December day when we spotted her. A ship sailing out of control, sails missing, others torn, being blown about on the Atlantic Ocean. The name of that ship was the *Mary Celeste*. And her story is the biggest mystery of the sea.

My name is Captain David Morehouse, and I am the captain of the ship that found the abandoned *Mary Celeste*. I want you to join me, to help me discover what happened.

To find out, let's go back to 1872, when the *Mary Celeste* set off on that fateful journey.

The Mystery of the Mary Celeste

Contents

1	Meet the narrator: Captain Morehouse	2
2	The *Mary Celeste*'s crew and their journey	4
3	Finding the *Mary Celeste*	8
4	Idea 1: Was it a seaquake?	20
5	Idea 2: Was it food poisoning?	24
6	Idea 3: Was it a sea monster?	28
7	Idea 4: Was it a waterspout?	32
8	Idea 5: Was it extra-terrestrial creatures?	34
9	Idea 6: Was it an explosion?	36
10	Idea 7: What about me?	40
	Glossary	44
	Index	45
	Discuss the arguments for and against each of the ideas	46

Written by Simon Yeend

Illustrated by Ludovic Salle

Collins